Nursery Rhymes

Preschool/Kindergarten

Save time and energy planning thematic units with this comprehensive resource. We've searched the 1985–1998 issues of **The MAILBOX®** and **Teacher's Helper®** magazines to find the best ideas for you to use when teaching a thematic unit about nursery rhymes. Included in this book are favorite units from the magazines, single ideas to extend a unit, and a variety of reproducible activities. Pick and choose from these activities to develop your own complete unit or simply to enhance your current lesson plans. You're sure to find everything you need for active learning fun.

Editors:
Angie Kutzer
Thad H. McLaurin
Michele M. Menzel

Artists:
Kimberly Richard
Donna K. Teal

Cover Artist:
Kimberly Richard

www.themailbox.com

Manufactured in the United States
10 9 8 7 6 5 4 3 2 1

Table Of Contents

Thematic Units

More Activities And Ideas

Reproducible Activities

Thematic Units...

from **The MAILBOX®** *magazine*

The Land Of Nursery Rhymes

Take your youngsters on an imaginative trip to the Land of Nursery Rhymes, and use these activities to supplement your traditional nursery-rhyme lesson plans. Soon your youngsters will be singing a song, putting on a play, making small books, creating a class book, and producing several crafts.

by Lucia Kemp Henry

Getting Ready For The Trip

Before your youngsters take off on an imaginary journey to the Land of Nursery Rhymes, organize a brainstorming session. Tell students that you will be pretending to visit Nursery-Rhyme Land. Ask them to think about what they might do in this imaginary place and who they might meet. Have your youngsters brainstorm presents to bring for each nursery-rhyme character as you list their suggestions on the board or chart paper. For example, students might suggest bringing a small pail for Jack and Jill, mittens for the three little kittens, a plastic spider for Miss Muffet, a toy horn for Little Boy Blue, and a candlestick for Jack (the nimble one). After completing the list and finding the items, have students pack them into a large suitcase or small trunk. Later give students opportunities to unpack and repack the items, recalling as they do the nursery-rhyme character with whom each item is associated.

We're On Our Way

Once the gifts are packed, it's time to be on the way to Nursery-Rhyme Land. Get students ready for the trip by saying this poem or converting it into a simple play with just a few props. (To create a role for each student, increase the number of Bo-Peep's sheep, add flower characters to go with Mary and her garden, or create additional spider characters to add to Miss Muffet's scene.) Have each student make his own costume by appropriately decorating a paper headband. If you have props nearby that would add to the flavor of the presentation, give them to the appropriate students. Then read the poem/play aloud as students dramatize their roles.

Afterward serve guests such delicacies as The Queen's Heart-Shaped Cookies, Humpty-Dumpty's Deviled Eggs, Peter Peter's Pumpkin Muffins, The Three Little Kittens' Pies, Twinkle's Star-Shaped Cheese Sandwiches, and Jack And Jill's Pail Of Punch.

Off We Go

Off we go to Nursery-Rhyme Land
And who do you think we'll see?
All of the folks from Nursery-Rhyme Land
Will be there with you and me!

Old King Cole will wear a great crown.
And Jack and Jill just might fall down!

Little Bo-Peep can bring her sheep,
While Little Boy Blue is fast asleep!

Twinkle the star will blink and shine.
Mary will tend her plants so fine.

Peter will show his pumpkin house.
We'll see a clock and climbing mouse.

Three small kittens will sigh and cry
While Humpty-Dumpty sits up high.

Lil' Miss Muffet will bring some whey.
Jack who's nimble will jump and play.

Cow from the moon will sing so sweet.
The Queen of Hearts will bake a treat!

It's time to say good-bye for now.
Nursery-rhyme folk, please take a bow!

by Lucia Kemp Henry

A Tour Of Nursery-Rhyme Land

Here's a cute foldout booklet that will be fun for your youngsters to make and read. Reproduce the booklet pages (pages 7–9) on white construction paper for each student. Have your youngsters trace the dashed lines on each of the pages for fine-motor practice, then color the pages and cut them out. Assist each youngster as he glues the pages together according to the directions. When the glue is dry, help youngsters accordion-fold their booklets. When the booklets are complete, encourage your youngsters to "read" them to other students or adults.

Nursery-Rhyme Book

Use the open reproducible on page 10 along with student-produced artwork to create a one-of-a-kind nursery-rhyme book. Ask each student to choose a different nursery rhyme to be the focus of his art. Write the nursery rhyme on a copy of page 10, and read it to the student before asking him to paint or draw a related picture on a 9" x 12" sheet of paper. Using a stapler that has a long reach, staple together sheets of 12" x 18" construction paper to create the pages of the book. Then glue each nursery rhyme beside the corresponding artwork. Have student volunteers title the book with your assistance and decorate the cover. This book will be a fine addition to your classroom library.

Take Your Pick

You'll find lots of ways to use the nursery-rhyme reproducible on page 10. One way to use the sheet is to reproduce it onto white construction paper and have each student personalize a copy to be glued on a nursery-rhyme folder or portfolio. You might want to use the design to accentuate a note to parents regarding your nursery-rhyme activities or to frame a class party invitation. Another way to use the sheet is to write a recipe that relates to your nursery-rhyme unit on the page before duplicating it. Then, as an optional assignment, send the recipe home and ask students to prepare the recipe with the assistance of an adult. Or, at the conclusion of your nursery-rhyme unit, make copies of the open design and write a positive comment on each one that relates to a particular student's involvement in the nursery-rhyme unit.

A Song To Sing Along The Way

Pick up the pace on your trip to the Land of Nursery Rhymes by teaching students this light-hearted song.

To Rhyming Land We Go!
(sung to the tune of
"The Farmer In The Dell")

To Rhyming Land we go,
To Rhyming Land we go!
High-ho the derry-o,
To Rhyming Land we go!

Continue singing the song as above, substituting the following verses:
Verse 2: King Cole wears a crown.
Verse 3: Jack and Jill fall down.
Verse 4: Bo-Peep has lost her sheep.
Verse 5: Boy Blue is fast asleep.
Verse 6: The cat can play a tune.
Verse 7: The cow jumps over the moon.
Verse 8: A star shines in the sky.
Verse 9: And now we'll say good-bye!

by Lucia Kemp Henry

Kittens From Bags

Make these cute bag puppets to use in dramatizing any reading of "The Three Little Kittens." Reproduce the bag puppet patterns on page 11 for each student. Have each youngster color and decorate his patterns as desired before cutting out the pieces. Demonstrate how to glue the patterns to a lunch bag to create a kitten puppet. (Provide assistance as necessary.) Glue the upper head pattern to what would normally be the bottom of the sack. Glue the lower head pattern underneath the flap created by the folded bag bottom. Glue the uncolored side of each mitten to the uncolored side of a paw. Glue the mitten-covered paws to the sides of the bag so that when they are extended outward the pads of the paws show, but when they are folded inward the mitten-covered sides of the paws show.

Give students an opportunity to dramatize "The Three Little Kittens" with their puppets as you read the nursery rhyme aloud. Show students how to stretch the kittens' paws outward during the parts of the rhyme that mention that the mittens are lost. Also show them how to fold the paws inward, revealing the mittens when you read the parts of the rhyme that mention that the mittens have been found.

Twinkle Star Headbands

This easy project will put stars in your youngsters' eyes and a lovely rhyme in their heads. Make a two-inch-wide, yellow construction-paper headband for each youngster. Have each student color and cut out copies of the star clusters and the two corresponding pattern pieces from page 12. Ask them to glue the cut-out pieces to opposite sides of the headband. Provide small sponge-printed star cutouts, construction-paper star cutouts, foil stars, and star stickers for youngsters to glue or stick on randomly in the empty spaces on their headbands. Encourage your students to wear their headbands as they march around singing the rhyme.

Glue to page 2 here.

Mary, Mary, quite contrary,
How does your garden grow?
With silver bells and cockleshells,
And pretty maids all in a row.

A Tour of
Nursery-Rhyme Land

Help Jack and Jill
find their friends
in Nursery-Rhyme Land!

Nursery-Rhyme Land Tour Booklet

Use with "A Tour Of Nursery-Rhyme Land" on page 5.

2

Glue to page 3 here.

Humpty-Dumpty sat on a wall.
Humpty-Dumpty had a great fall;
All the King's horses and
All the King's men
Couldn't put Humpty together again.

©The Education Center, Inc. • *Nursery Rhymes* • Preschool/Kindergarten • TEC3173

Jack be nimble,
Jack be quick,
Jack jump over
The candlestick.

3

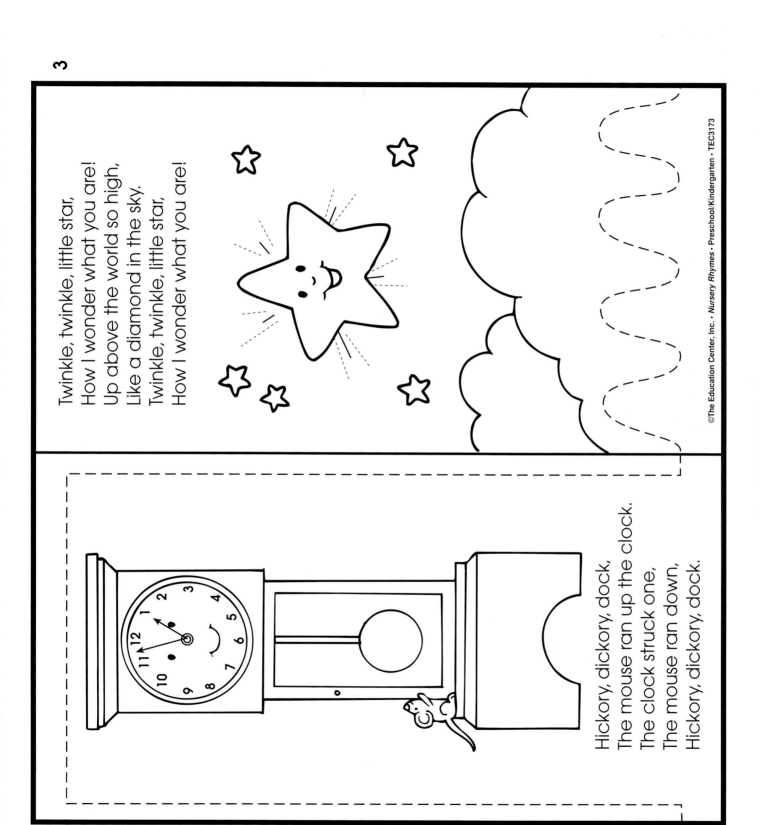

Twinkle, twinkle, little star,
How I wonder what you are!
Up above the world so high,
Like a diamond in the sky.
Twinkle, twinkle, little star,
How I wonder what you are!

Hickory, dickory, dock,
The mouse ran up the clock.
The clock struck one,
The mouse ran down,
Hickory, dickory, dock.

Nursery Rhymes Open Sheet

Use with "Take Your Pick" and "Nursery-Rhyme Book" on page 5.

©The Education Center, Inc. • *Nursery Rhymes* • Preschool/Kindergarten • TEC3173

finished project

upper head

lower head

paws

mittens

fold

fold

Glue this part to the side of the bag.

Glue this part to the side of the bag.

Star Patterns

Use with "Twinkle Star Headbands" on page 6.

finished project

Twinkle, twinkle, little star. How I wonder what you are.

Up above the world so high, Like a diamond in the sky.

Hey Diddle, Diddle!

Hey diddle, diddle!
The cat and the fiddle;
The cow jumped over the moon.
The little dog laughed
To see such sport,
And the dish ran away with the spoon.

What's more likely to capture your youngsters' imaginations than a curiously musical cat, a fantastically high-flying cow, a laughing dog, and a pair of unlikely tableware runaways? It's a fact—this fantasy provides lots of learning fun!

by Lucia Kemp Henry

Fantastic Fantasy Pairs

Your youngsters are sure to detect some make-believe as they meet the characters in "Hey Diddle, Diddle." Prior to introducing the rhyme, enlarge and duplicate page 15; then cut out each pattern along the bold and dotted lines to create eight separate pieces. Prepare each piece for use on a flannelboard. During a group time, give each cutout to a different student. Recite Lines One and Two of the rhyme; then ask the children holding the cat and fiddle pieces to put them on the flannelboard. Repeat these steps for Line Three *(cow, moon)*. After reciting Lines Four and Five, explain that the dog needs the telescope in order to see all the fun; then ask the children holding those items to put them on the flannelboard. Finally repeat the steps for Line Six *(dish, spoon)*. When you've finished the rhyme, ask volunteers to tell why they think the characters are more make-believe than real.

Fact Or Fantasy?

Continue your investigation of real and make-believe with this up-and-down listening game. Read each of the questions below. Direct your children to stand up to answer a question "yes" and to sit down to indicate "no."

Can a cat meow?
Can a cat play a fiddle?

Can a cow eat grass?
Can a cow jump over the moon?

Can a dog wag its tail?
Can a dog laugh?

Can a dish and a spoon be washed?
Can a dish and a spoon run away?

Hey Diddle, Diddle; The Cat And The Fiddle

Through this activity, your youngsters will discover that music and art make great partners. Invite each child to fingerpaint while listening to country-fiddle or classical-violin music. When each child's fiddle-inspired painting is dry, have her further decorate it with cat stickers. Fiddling around with paint and music is the cat's meow!

The Cow Jumped Over The Moon

Watch your little ones jump for joy when you invite them to make moon-shaped cookies. In advance bake a batch of crescent moon–shaped cookies. (Use a cookie cutter and your favorite sugar-cookie recipe. Or cut refrigerated cookie dough into slices; then cut away a portion of one side of each slice.) To prepare a cookie treat, a child spreads white frosting onto a cookie, then adds yellow sugar sprinkles. Finally he adds a candy-corn nose and a mini-chocolate-chip eye.

The Little Dog Laughed To See Such Sport

Ask your children what the little dog saw that made him laugh out loud, and they'll quickly remind you of the cow jumping over a moon. Then expand children's thinking by asking them to think of scenes involving an animal other than the cow that would tickle the little dog's funny bone—scenes such as a pig in a bubble bath or an elephant on the slide. Direct each child to draw his own silly scene; then have him dictate a sentence to describe the laughable action. Enlarge the dog character and his telescope (page 15); then mount it along with the children's pictures and the caption "The little dog laughed to see such sport!" Your youngsters are sure to laugh, as well, when they see the sights they've imagined!

The Dish Ran Away With The Spoon

Invite students to pair up at this center to match the dishes and spoons that would be most likely to run away together. To make this matching game, program a number of plastic-plate and plastic-spoon pairs with matching stickers. Store the programmed tableware in a dish rack in the center along with a colorful tablecloth so that youngsters are inspired to set a table with all the dish-and-spoon duos they can find.

Real Partners In Learning

Both parent and child will have a fantastic time when paired up to play this take-home game. Duplicate two copies of page 15 and one copy of page 16 for each child. Have each child color his shape patterns, then cut them out. Cut each of the eight shapes in half where indicated. Have the child color, cut out, and glue the poem to a personalized, colorful paper bag and then attach star stickers. Tuck the 16 shape patterns and the parent note/directions inside the bag. Families and learning fun—now that's a match!

Hey diddle, diddle;
The cat and the fiddle,
The cow jumped over the moon.
The little dog laughed
To see such sport,
And the dish ran away with the spoon.

Shelly

Use with "Fantastic Fantasy Pairs" on page 13 and "The Little Dog
Laughed To See Such Sport" and "Real Partners In Learning" on page 14.

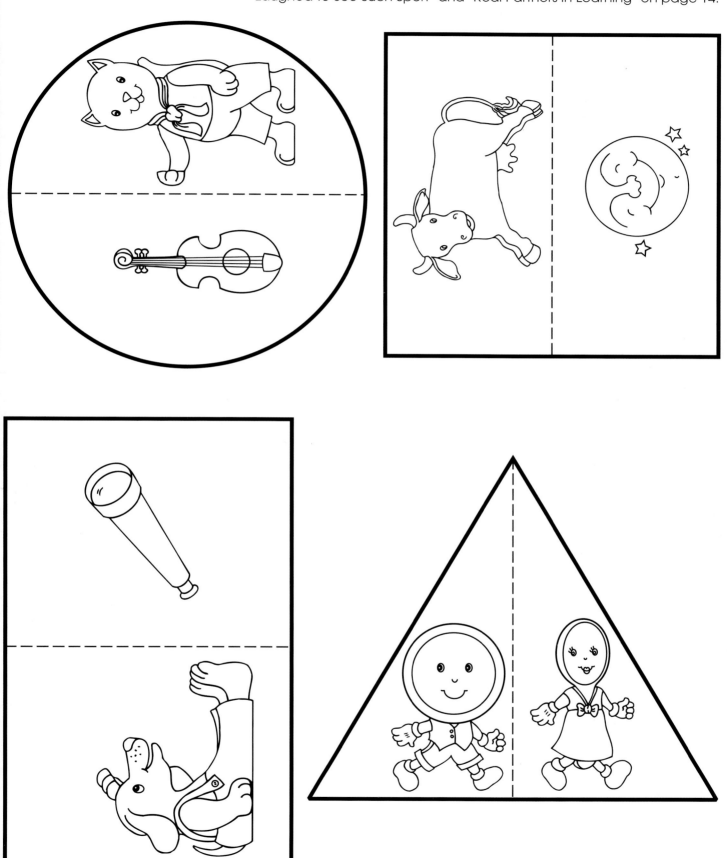

Patterns

Use with "Real Partners In Learning" on page 14.

Parent Note

Dear Parent,

Both you and your child will have a fantastic time when you pair up to play this game. First review the nursery rhyme on the bag. Then put the bag with the 16 game pieces inside between you and your child.

To begin play, take one game piece out of the bag and put it faceup in front of you. Have your child do the same. Then take out a second piece. If that piece is not a shape match to your first piece, put it back in the bag. If the piece is a shape match, keep it. Have your child take a second piece in the same manner. Continue in this manner until either you or your child has four pairs of different shapes. The first person to have a complete set of four pairs recites the rhyme.

Hey diddle, diddle!

The cat and the fiddle;

The cow jumped over the moon.

The little dog laughed

To see such sport,

And the dish ran away with the spoon.

Jack Be Nimble; Jill Be Quick

It's time to update the classic nursery rhyme about jumping Jack and his candlestick. These activities for Jacks *and* Jills will fill your classroom with active learners!

Jack Be Nimble—And Jill Jump, Too!

To prepare for this activity, duplicate the patterns on page 21. Color the candles (or duplicate on colored construction paper) and prepare them for use on a flannelboard. Invite youngsters to help you modify the original rhyme as you place different colors, numbers, and sizes of candles on your flannelboard (see the candle below). Then place the pieces and the board in a center for children to enjoy independently.

Jack be nimble. Jack be quick.
Jack jump over the candlestick.

Jill be nimble. Jill be quick.
Jill jump over the candlestick.

Jack be nimble. Jack be quick.
Jack jump over **two** candlesticks.

Jill be nimble. Jill be quick.
Jill jump over the **red** candlestick.

Jack be nimble. Jack be quick.
Jack jump over the **tall** candlestick.

Jumping Jacks And Jills

Get youngsters' legs, feet, arms, and hands moving with this bouncy song. Your children will jolly well enjoy jumping along!

The Jumping Song
(sung to the tune of "B-I-N-G-O")

Let's jump up and down right now,
'Cause jumping's lots of fun, oh!
Jump! Jump! Jump! Jump! Jump!
Jump! Jump! Jump! Jump! Jump!
Jump! Jump! Jump! Jump! Jump!
Oh, jumping's lots of fun, oh!

Let's jump with our arms out
  wide…
Let's jump with our arms up
  high…
Let's jump with our hands on
  heads….
Let's jump with our hands on
  hips…

—Lucia Kemp Henry

This Little Light Of Mine

Youngsters will jump at the chance to make these candle look-alikes. To make one, use tempera paint to paint a cardboard tube. When the paint is dry, decorate the tube using additional paint or seasonal stickers. Personalize the candle. Gently crumple a ten-inch square of yellow or orange tissue paper; then tape the paper inside the tube to resemble a flame. If desired, spray the tissue-paper flame with adhesive glitter, or dribble glue over the flame and sprinkle on glitter. Arrange the candles in a window, or use them with the following activities.

Jump For Joy!

Keep your little jitterbugs jumping, jiggling, and generally wiggling with this movement activity. Seat youngsters in an open area; then ask them to brainstorm additional ways that Jack could move over or around the candlestick, such as *march*, *run*, or *slide*. Write each movement word on a separate index card. Also write each child's name on an index card. Place the sets of cards in separate containers. Provide each child with his candle (see "This Little Light Of Mine"). From the two containers, select a movement card and a name card. (If desired, display the selected cards in a pocket chart.) Then ask the child whose name was chosen to place his candle on the floor for the group to admire. Encourage him to move over or around the candle in the suggested manner as the group chants the rhyme, substituting the child's name and the movement. Return the movement card to the container. Play until each child has been featured in the activity.

Rodney
march

Leaps And Bounds

Your little ones will be as nimble as Jack when they participate in this simple but fun musical activity. Randomly arrange the children's candles (see "This Little Light Of Mine") on the floor in an open area of your room, making sure there is plenty of room for jumping over the candles. Direct the children to dance freely about the room—jumping over candles in their paths—as you play a lively instrumental selection.

Once the children have warmed up, try this variation that emphasizes listening skills as well as spatial awareness. Ask each child to stand beside his own candle. Designate a group to pick up their candles and dance and jump about the room as the music plays. For example, ask the Jacks (boys) only or the Jills (girls) only to move. Or request that those children with a specific color of candle dance. Everyone is sure to have some hot movement fun!

Your little Jacks and Jills will delight in making their own candles at this supervised center. Half-fill a coffee can with cold water. Place about one pound of household paraffin wax and some crayon pieces in a second, identically sized coffee can. Half-fill a pot of water; then bring it to a boil. Place the can of wax in the water. Stir the wax as it melts. When the wax has melted, place the can along with the can of water onto a work surface that has been protected with newspaper. For each child, cut a length of heavy cotton string so that it is slightly longer than the height of the can. Tie the string to one of the rounded corners of a clothes hanger. Direct the child to hold the opposite end of the clothes hanger as he repeatedly dips his string alternately into the wax, then into the cold water. When the candle is the desired width, flatten the bottom of the warm candle by pressing it onto the tabletop. Cut the candle off the string, leaving enough string for a wick.

If desired, provide each child with a ball of clay or Crayola® Model Magic®. Direct him to shape the clay into a candleholder. Encourage youngsters to present their candles and holders as gifts to loved ones.

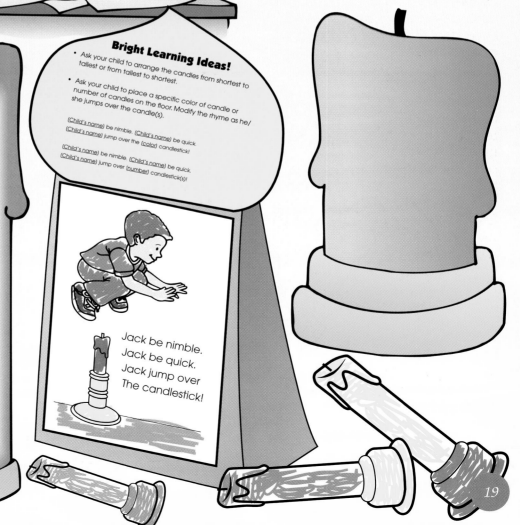

Luminous Learning

These take-home projects will shed some light on the ease with which parents can help youngsters learn at home. For each child, duplicate a copy of the parent note (on page 20) onto yellow paper. Duplicate a set of candles and the nursery-rhyme pattern (pages 20 and 21) onto white construction paper. Cut out the note and patterns. Direct each child to color the nursery-rhyme pattern, then glue it to a personalized paper bag. Direct her to color each of her candles a different color. Place the candles in her bag; then fold down the top of the bag. Tape the parent note to the top of the bag; then tape the bag closed. Have each child take her bag home for some family fun.

Bright Learning Ideas!

- Ask your child to arrange the candles from shortest to tallest or from tallest to shortest.

- Ask your child to place a specific color of candle or number of candles on the floor. Modify the rhyme as he/she jumps over the candle(s).

(Child's name) be nimble. (Child's name) be quick.
(Child's name) jump over the (color) candlestick!

(Child's name) be nimble. (Child's name) be quick.
(Child's name) jump over (number) candlestick(s)!

Jack be nimble.
Jack be quick.
Jack jump over
The candlestick!

Parent Note

Use with "Luminous Learning" on page 19.

Bright Learning Ideas!

- Ask your child to arrange the candles from shortest to tallest or from tallest to shortest.

- Ask your child to place a specific color of candle or number of candles on the floor. Modify the rhyme as he/she jumps over the candle(s).

(Child's name) be nimble. (Child's name) be quick.
(Child's name) jump over the (color) candlestick!

(Child's name) be nimble. (Child's name) be quick.
(Child's name) jump over (number) candlestick(s)!

Nursery-Rhyme Pattern

Use with "Luminous Learning" on page 19.

Jack be nimble.
Jack be quick.
Jack jump over
The candlestick!

Use with "Jack Be Nimble—And Jill Jump, Too!" on page 17 and "Luminous Learning" on page 19.

Mary, Mary, How Does Your Garden Grow?

Come into the garden to see how Mary's rows of lovely flowers grow! Use the ideas in this unit with your little ones and you're sure to sow some seeds of learning.

by Lucia Kemp Henry

Mary's Gorgeous Garden Rows

How does Mary's garden grow? In rows, of course! Duplicate the patterns on page 25; then cut out and prepare Mary and her garden for use on a flannelboard. Display Mary and the rows of flowers as you introduce the rhyme so that your youngsters discover just how neat a gardener Mary is. Identify the silver bells, cockleshells, and pretty maids. Then ask volunteers to share why they think Mary is so contrary.

Fabulous Faux Flowers

The next best thing to Mary's own garden blossoms are the flowers that your little ones make to accompany the following rhyme. To make a flower puppet, glue a Styrofoam®-ball half onto a paper bag; then add a paper stem, leaves, and flower petals. Glue wiggle eyes onto the Styrofoam® ball. Reinforce the size concepts presented in this poem by displaying the tall, medium-sized, and short flowers from page 25. Then invite each child to slip his puppet over his hand and to participate in the following action poem. Keep Mary's figure nearby so she can keep an eye on her flowers, no matter what their size.

Flowers All In A Row

Children: Mary, Mary, tell us, Mary! How does your garden grow?
Teacher: I bought a lot of pretty flowers and planted each kind in a row.
Children with puppets line up in a row.

Children: Mary, Mary, tell us, Mary! How does your garden grow?
Teacher: I planted all the **big, tall** flowers in a nice, straight row.
Children hold puppets up high.

Children: Mary, Mary, tell us, Mary! How does your garden grow?
Teacher: I planted all the **medium-sized** flowers in a nice, straight row.
Children hold puppets at chest level.

Children: Mary, Mary, tell us, Mary! How does your garden grow?
Teacher: I planted all the **small, short** flowers in a nice, straight row.
Children hold puppets at knee level.

Sand Table Flower Garden

Challenge youngsters to plant flowers of all heights and sizes right in your sand table. Enhance your sand center with small plastic shovels, empty yogurt containers, and a basket of inexpensive, fake flowers in three different heights. (Trim the stems of the flowers, if necessary.) As your little gardeners plant pots and rows of flowers, demonstrate how to compare the sizes of the flowers using words such as *big, tall, tallest, short, shorter, shortest,* and so forth.

Flower Garden

How did your youngsters' sand table garden grow? Did it bloom with colorful faux blossoms? Follow up their dramatic play by reading aloud *Flower Garden* by Eve Bunting (Harcourt Brace & Company). As you read, point out the steps the girl takes in creating her garden, from putting the "garden in a shopping cart" to putting the "garden in a window box." After reading, take your youngsters on a visit to a garden center to see and smell all the flowers they'll find there. If a trip is not possible, purchase a bunch of inexpensive flowers from a florist. Give your budding flower specialists plenty of time to observe the blossoms with their eyes and noses; then invite floral descriptions blooming with special scents and wonderful colors.

Colorful Flowers Game

Prepare this simple game for partners that looks like the container of colorful flowers that the girl in *Flower Garden* prepared for her mother. To prepare the game, obtain a large, six-section, plastic seedling container from a nursery; six 2 1/2-inch Styrofoam® eggs; five artificial flowers (red, blue, yellow, purple, and orange); and a green leaf stem. Paint each Styrofoam® egg one of the six colors. When the paint is dry, hot-glue each egg—wide end up—into a section of the container. Use a pencil to poke a hole into each egg. Cut a construction-paper square in each of the six colors. To play, each partner in turn draws a square, says the color, and then puts the matching flower or leaf stem into the corresponding section of the container. Wow! What pretty flowers you planted together!

Sing A Colorful Song

Continue the emphasis on colorful flowers and how they grow by teaching your little ones this song. Distribute one red, orange, yellow, blue, or purple artificial flower to each child in the group. Encourage the children to move their flowers as suggested. Sing the final two lines of the song slowly, encouraging each youngster to hold up her flower as its color is mentioned.

Sing A Song Of Flowers
(sung to the tune of "Sing A Song Of Sixpence")

Sing a song of flowers, flowers all around.	*Wave flower.*
Flowers that are growing, growing in the ground.	*Hold flower near ground.*
Flowers of each color make a pretty view.	*Hold flower in front of eyes.*
Red and orange and yellow,	*Hold flower above head.*
And blue and purple, too!	

Plant A Garden Of Home Learning

Prepare this flower-themed activity to send home with each child for a special home delivery of learning fun. To assemble a game bag for each child, have a child color a copy of the patterns on page 25. Cut out the patterns; then glue Mary onto a colorful paper bag. Personalize the bag. Tuck the flower patterns and parent note (page 26) inside the bag. If desired, fold the top of the bag down once; then punch two holes side by side through the thicknesses. Insert an artificial flower's stem through the holes, securing it with tape, if necessary. Mary's rhymes and flowers are sure to help your youngsters' home learning experiences grow!

Patterns

Use with "Mary's Gorgeous Garden Rows" and "Fabulous Faux Flowers" on page 22 and "Plant A Garden Of Home Learning" on page 24.

Mary, Mary, quite contrary,
How does your garden grow?
With silver bells and cockleshells,
And pretty maids all in a row.

Dear Parent,

Mary and her rows of flowers are sure to help you and your child grow a garden of learning fun! To play, lay the bag flat on a table along with the flowers. Review the traditional rhyme as shown on the bag. Then recite a verse of the modified rhyme below, inserting your child's name. Ask your child to find the three flowers that match the description in that verse, and to arrange the flowers in a row. Continue in the same manner for each verse until all three sizes of flowers are "planted" in nice, straight rows.

(Child's name), (Child's name), tell me, (Child's name),
How does your garden grow?
My very special garden grows
With **tall** flowers in a row.

(Child's name), (Child's name), tell me, (Child's name),
How does your garden grow?
My very special garden grows
With **short** flowers in a row.

(Child's name), (Child's name), tell me, (Child's name),
How does your garden grow?
My very special garden grows
With **medium** flowers in a row.

Jack Be Nimble			
5			
4			candle
3		candle	candle
2	candle	candle	candle
1	candle	candle	candle

Jack's Candles

Your youngsters will jump at the chance to work together on this graphing exercise. Duplicate the graph shown for each student. Then create a poster board enlargement of the graph. Provide assorted colors of candles or candle cutouts (not to exceed five of one color). Have students work in small groups to place the candles by color on the large graph. Then have each student color one block on his personal graph for each candle of the same color on the poster board graph.

Susan Puckett—Gr. K,
Pearl Lower Elementary
Pearl, MS

Scurry Around The Clock

Use this hurry-scurry movement activity to reinforce numeral recognition. In advance prepare a large clock face on the floor. Using a plastic hoop as a guide, mark a circle on the floor with colored tape. Next cut the numerals from 1 through 12 out of colorful Con-Tact® covering. Attach them to the floor inside the circle outline to create a clock's face. Invite a child to join you by the clock. Create a mouse-head-shaped cutout for each student. Use a hole puncher to make two holes in the top of each cutout. Then attach the cutout to one of the child's shoes by stringing his shoelace through the two holes. Count aloud as you strike a block from 1 to 12 times. Encourage the child to scurry clockwise around the clock until the mouse on his shoe has landed on the appropriate numeral. Once familiar with the game, pair students so that one child strikes the block while the other scurries around the clock.

Treasure Hunt

A nursery rhyme unit is so much fun, it deserves a finale that's equally entertaining. Collect several items which could be related to the nursery rhymes your students know. For example, a plastic spider could be the eensy-weensy spider; a sprig of silk flowers could represent the garden of Mary, Mary quite contrary; an egg-shaped hosiery container could represent Humpty Dumpty; and three small paper bags, stuffed with shredded newspaper, could represent the wool of the black sheep. If you want your last item to be a snack, provide a pie or two representing the one the three little kittens had. Hide each item along with a clue card that will lead youngsters to the next item. Remember to put your edible treat last. Keep the clue card for the first item yourself. To start the treasure hunt, read the first clue card aloud. Working together students locate the item, determine the rhyme to which it relates, and say the rhyme in unison. They then use the clue they found to continue to the next item. Won't they be surprised when they actually get to eat the last item! "Meow, meow, meow!"

Denise Hazlerigs
Hodge Elementary School
Denton, TX

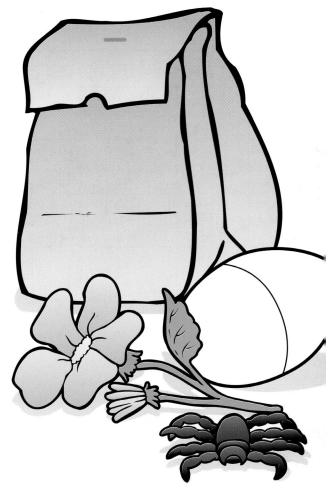

Poetry Cubes

It's rhyme time with these poetry cubes. To make a cube, trim two paper milk cartons to the same height and insert the open end of one carton into the open end of the other carton. Cover the cube with colored paper or Con-Tact® covering. Write poems on squares of paper cut slightly smaller than a side of the cube. To illustrate each poem, attach a sticker or draw a related picture. Attach one poem to each side of the cube. Make a variety of poetry cubes, each with a different emphasis—all nursery rhymes or birthday poems, for example. To begin your rhyming fun, ask a child to toss a cube; then as a class recite the poem that is on top. Keep the cubes handy, to be used during transitions or as time fillers.

Bobbie Hallman, Burbank School, Merced, CA

Where Is Little Boy Blue?

What if Little Boy Blue wasn't under the haystack, but over it or behind it instead? Then you'd definitely have a great excuse to work with positional concepts. To make a haystack, cut a haystack shape from tagboard. Coat the haystack with a layer of glue; then sprinkle on bits of straw, hay, or crushed Shredded Wheat. Allow this to dry. Color and cut out a likeness of Little Boy Blue. Once each of your youngsters has created his own haystack and Little Boy Blue, call out positional phrases and have students position their boy cutouts around their haystacks to match.

Tressella Benson—Gr. K, Lowell School, Louisville, KY

Little Boy Blue's Haystacks

This follow-up activity for use with "Little Boy Blue" is sure to give haystacks a sweet reputation. Assist children as they make this snack. Melt two packages of butterscotch chips on a hot plate or in a microwave. Do not stir. Mix a large package of chow mein noodles with the melted butterscotch chips. Drop spoonfuls of this mixture onto waxed paper to cool. Serve these mouth-watering haystacks for snack.

Jane Nash—Gr. K, Pearl Lower Elementary, Pearl, MS

Itsy-Bitsy Puppet

Make a puppet to use while singing the favorite song "The Itsy-Bitsy Spider." From felt, cut a sun shape and a cloud shape small enough to fit inside a paper cup. Glue the shapes, back-to-back, on one end of a pipe cleaner. Wrap one end of a second pipe cleaner around a plastic spider that is also small enough to fit inside the cup. Punch two small holes in the bottom of the paper cup. Insert the pipe cleaners through the holes so that the shapes and the spider are hidden inside the cup. As you sing, slide the pipe cleaners up and down, revealing the corresponding shapes. Youngsters will want to sing the song over and over again when moving their very own itsy-bitsy spider puppets.

Karen Naylor—Pre-K
Palmer Preschool, Salem, NH

Jack and Jill's Science Center

The rhyme doesn't tell us whether Jack and Jill eventually got water from the well. But you'll definitely want to fill a pail with water for this science center. Provide several objects that will sink and several that will float. For each object, make a matching picture card. Create two poster-board pail cutouts. Label one "sink" and one "float."

To use the center, a student places the objects one-by-one into the pail of water. Observing the results, he then places the corresponding card on the appropriate pail.

Jane Nash—Gr. K

Twinkle, Twinkle, Little Star

Set your youngsters aglow with interest using this visual memory game. Recite "Twinkle, Twinkle, Little Star" with your youngsters. Then place eight to ten different-colored star cutouts on a tabletop. Give youngsters plenty of time to analyze what's on the table. Ask students to close their eyes as you remove one or more of the stars. Then give students opportunities to guess which color(s) is missing.

Vary this game for other nursery rhymes by changing the cutouts to match elements from the rhymes.

Laurie Atkinson—Gr. K
A.S. Johnston
Irving, TX

How Does Your Garden Grow?

Mary, Mary is quite contrary. But none of your youngsters will be when you ask them to create these whimsical watering cans. If desired, create a gardening mood for this project by wearing a large flowered hat and surrounding yourself with flowering potted plants. To make a watering can, trace a pattern onto construction paper and cut it out. Decorate the can using crayons or paints. Be certain to put a few dots on the spout. Then attach assorted foil or iridescent ribbon lengths atop the dots to resemble water pouring out of the holes in the spout.

Elsa Hoffman—Gr. K, Riverview School, Denville, NJ

Little Miss Muffet's Spider Count

Your youngsters will have lots of creepy counting fun as they prepare these individual counting booklets. Fold four sheets of paper in half and staple them to create an eight-page booklet. Decorate the cover, add a title, and write your name. Open the booklet and number each page sequentially. Starting with page one, make a set of spiders to match the number. To make a spider's body, press your thumb onto a black ink pad and then onto the booklet page. Use a fine-tip marker to add legs and other details to the fingerprint body. When this booklet is complete, everyone can have a good laugh as they flip the pages counting spiders and improving their math skills.

Susan Puckett—Gr. K
Pearl Lower Elementary
Pearl, MS

In And Out Of The Web

Although this is a game Little Miss Muffet would have shied away from, your little ones are likely to be drawn to it like bugs to a web. Make a spinner gameboard similar to the one shown. For spiderwebs, glue a real berry basket near each corner. Each player is given four spider rings to start play. In turn, each child spins and puts a spider in his basket or takes one out of his basket as directed by the spinner. Play continues until one player has all four of his spiders in his basket.

Jane Nash—Gr. K

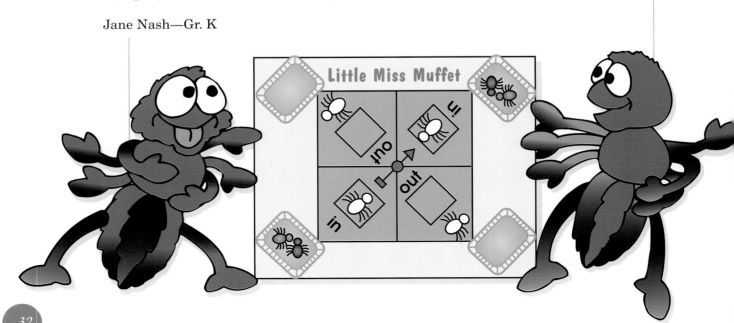

Reciting Rhymes

Students can learn to recite an assortment of nursery rhymes at this listening center. At the center set up a listening station and display a visual clue such as a picture card or a poster for each nursery rhyme you plan to feature. Prepare a recording to be used in the center in the following manner: First reveal the title of the upcoming rhyme and ask students to find a matching picture card in the center. Next invite students to listen carefully to the rhyme you will read; then read the rhyme. Follow this reading with an invitation to recite the rhyme with you as you complete a second reading. Continue in this manner, taping the desired number of rhymes. Students will soon be reciting the rhymes without the aid of the listening center! Program new tapes as needed.

This little **went to** [church] **.**

This little **stayed home.**

This little **had**  **.**

This little **had none.**

This little [pig] **cried,**

Wee, wee, wee! [pig]

All the way home!

Ruff, ruff, ruff! [dog]

Mixed-Up Rhymes

Take advantage of your students' love of nursery rhymes as you develop their creative thinking skills. Choose a nursery rhyme and identify its key words. Write the rhyme on an experience chart using rebus pictures to replace the key words as shown in the illustration. Have your students think of words to replace the rebus pictures. Draw their suggestions on small cards and have them place each card in the appropriate place on the chart. When you're finished, you'll have an original rhyme and a room of proud poets.

Karen Martin—Gr. K
Hahira Elementary School
Hahira, GA

Playing The Part

Set aside a day for students to dress as their favorite nursery rhyme characters. In advance, notify parents of this special event, so they can help their youngsters plan their costumes. Some students may need to make their dress-up plans at school. Pair these students with older students. Together they can collect the neccessary props and costumes. On the specified day, parade to neighboring classes and snack on rhyme-related treats.

Susan Brown—Gr. K
Willis Elentary School
Willis, VA

A Bag Of Nursery Rhymes

Turn your nursery-rhyme recitations into a time of challenge and fun for students. Fill a colorful cloth bag with items to represent different nursery rhymes. For instance, use a candle for "Jack Be Nimble," a plastic egg for "Humpty Dumpty," and an artificial flower for "Mary, Mary, Quite Contrary." Ask a student to reach into the bag and remove one object. Have him name the rhyme he thinks is represented by that object. Then have the student or the entire class say the rhyme together. For an additional challenge, have a student feel, then—without looking at it—describe the object. When his classmates correctly guess the object, they may recite the corresponding rhyme.

Cathy Mansfield—Preschool
The Playstation
Trucksville, PA

Humpty-Dumpty Day

Who would think that a hard-boiled egg could be so much fun? Try the activities below with your little ones; then follow the recipe at the right for a tasty treat.

- Read and recite "Humpty-Dumpty."
- Identify the rhyming words in the poem.
- Place eggs on a wall; then make them fall off the wall.
- Discuss position words and opposites.
- Name the shape and colors of the egg and its parts.
- Introduce/reinforce vocabulary: cracked, oval, half, egg white, egg yolk, wire whisk.
- Follow the recipe and cook!

Judy Lawrence—Gr. K
Ascension Catholic Primary
Donaldsonville, LA

Deviled Eggs

1 hard-boiled egg per child
1 large bottle Thousand Island salad
   dressing

Peel the shell off each egg. Cut each egg in half lengthwise. Put all of the yolks in a bowl; then chop them with a wire whisk. Stir in salad dressing until the mixture is creamy. Spoon the mixture into the egg whites. Arrange the eggs on a plate and serve.

"Baa, Baa"

This black sheep looks as though he's wearing three bags of wool. To make imitation wool, shake cotton balls in a Ziploc bag with powdered black tempera paint. As you remove each cotton ball from the bag, shake it to remove the excess powder. Then glue several of these dark cotton balls to a sheep cutout. "Yes, sir. Yes, sir. It looks like three bags full to me!"

Susan Puckett—Gr. K

Building A Wall

Humpty Dumpty is the inspiration for this visual-discrimination game. Select and trace several wooden blocks as though to form a wall on a 9" x 12" sheet of tagboard. Color the resulting spaces to match the blocks. Draw Humpty Dumpty above the wall, color him, and laminate the tagboard. To use the game, a student reproduces the wall directly below or atop the traced outlines. No doubt that's one of the finer walls Humpty Dumpty has ever fallen from.

Jane Nash—Gr. K

Crackled Humpty Dumpty

All the king's horses and all the king's men couldn't keep your youngsters from falling for this Humpty Dumpty likeness. To make this project, coat a tagboard oval cutout with thinned glue. Then cover the glue with crushed eggshells or bits of white tissue paper. Once the glue has dried, attach wiggle eyes and create additional features if desired.

Tressella Benson—Gr. K
Lowell School
Louisville, KY

To Banbury Cross

If your youngsters have been reciting "Ride A Cock-Horse To Banbury Cross," they're going to have a ball with this frolicking musical idea. For this activity, you will need craft loops (often made into pot holders, ask for them at arts-and-crafts stores) and jingle bells (at least two per child). Slip one end of the loop through the opening of the jingle bell. Insert the other loop end into the first one and pull to hold the bell snugly. Repeat this until each bell is attached to a loop. Have each of your youngsters take off his shoes and socks and wrap at least one bell on a big toe and one on a finger. Have your youngsters dance and jump around so they'll have music wherever they go.

Betty Silkunas, Lansdale, PA

Reproducible Activities...

Background for the Teacher:

Over half of the 800 or so poems we call nursery rhymes are well over 200 years old. Frenchman Charles Perrault published the first collection in 1697, called <u>Tales of Mother Goose</u>. The first American version appeared in 1794. The oral traditions of these rhymes extend to every European country, and some even exist in African and Asian versions.

There are six basic categories of nursery rhymes: lullabies, play rhymes ("Patty Cake"), number rhymes, history rhymes ("The Brave Old Duke Of York"), cumulative rhymes ("The House That Jack Built") and riddles.

Extension Activities:

• Emphasize the rhythm of a nursery rhyme with a choral reading, complete with rhythm instruments.

• Pack an old suitcase with items associated with different nursery rhyme characters. Have students guess the character for each item.

• Make a number bulletin board featuring nursery rhymes that mention numbers: "Three Blind Mice," "Seven Wives of St. Ives," etc. Students draw the correct number of pictures to illustrate each rhyme.

• For a life-sized art project, trace body shapes on foamcore board (available in hobby, art and hardware stores) or cardboard. Have children paint costumes for different nursery rhyme characters on the outlines. Cut out face holes so students can put themselves in the picture. Have your instant camera ready!

Finished Sample

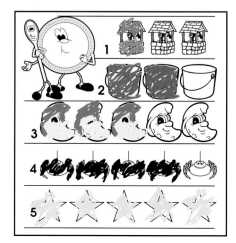

A Spoonful Of Sets

Color pictures in each set to equal the number.

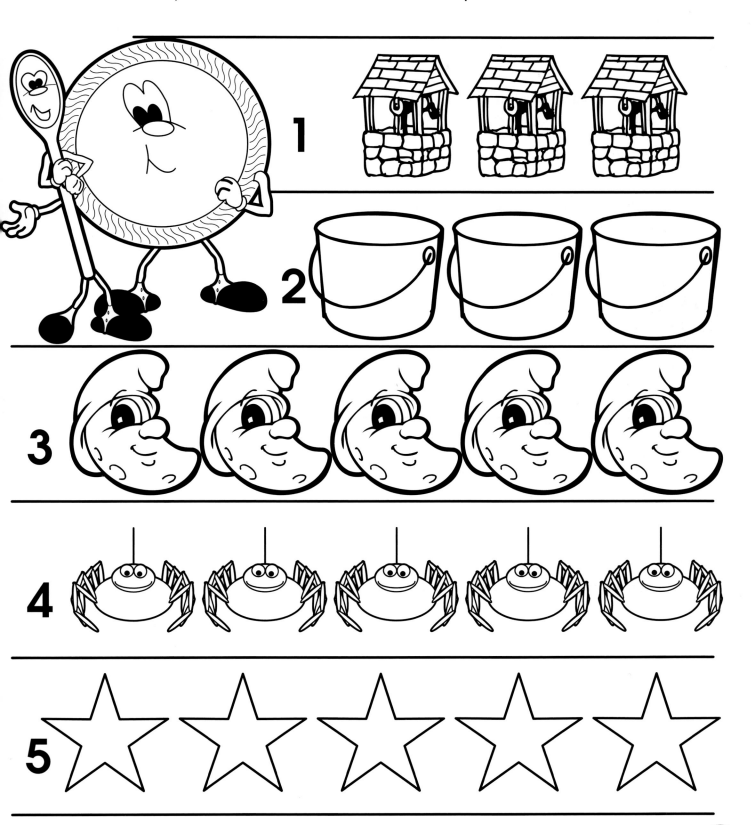

1

2

3

4

5

How To Use Page 41

Before directing students to complete page 41, read aloud the letters in each pumpkin in the example. Then have students locate and color the pumpkin containing two letters that are the same.

Finished Sample

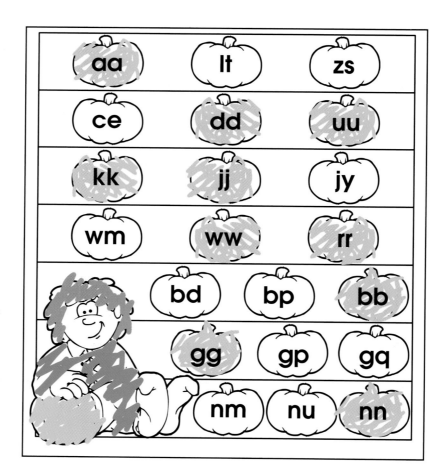

Name _____

Peter Peter Pumpkin Pairs

Color the pumpkin orange if the letters are the same.

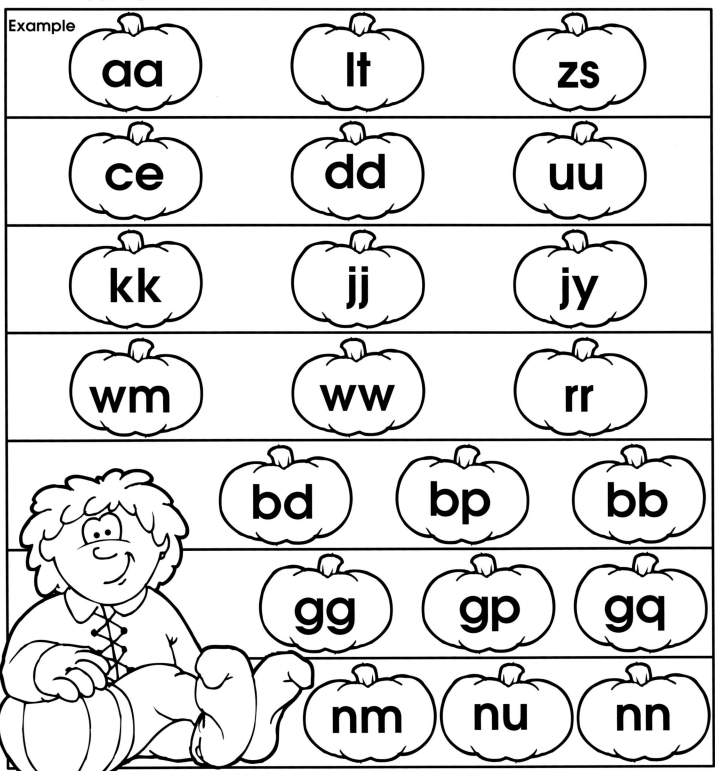

Example

aa	lt	zs
ce	dd	uu
kk	jj	jy
wm	ww	rr
bd	bp	bb
gg	gp	gq
nm	nu	nn

How To Use Page 43

1. Duplicate the page for each child.
2. Using the directions below (or create your own), have your youngsters listen to and follow the directions to prepare the activity.
   - *Point to the first coin at the bottom of this sheet.*
   - *What coin is it?*
   - *This is a nickel. A real nickel is gray. A nickel is the same as 5¢.*
   - *Color the nickel gray.*
   - *Point to the second coin at the bottom.*
   - *What coin is it?*
   - *This is a penny. A penny is brown. A penny is the same as 1¢.*
   - *Color the penny brown.*
   - *Color the other three coins correctly.*
3. Read aloud the directions on page 43 and encourage students to complete the page.

Finished Sample

Penny For The Pieman

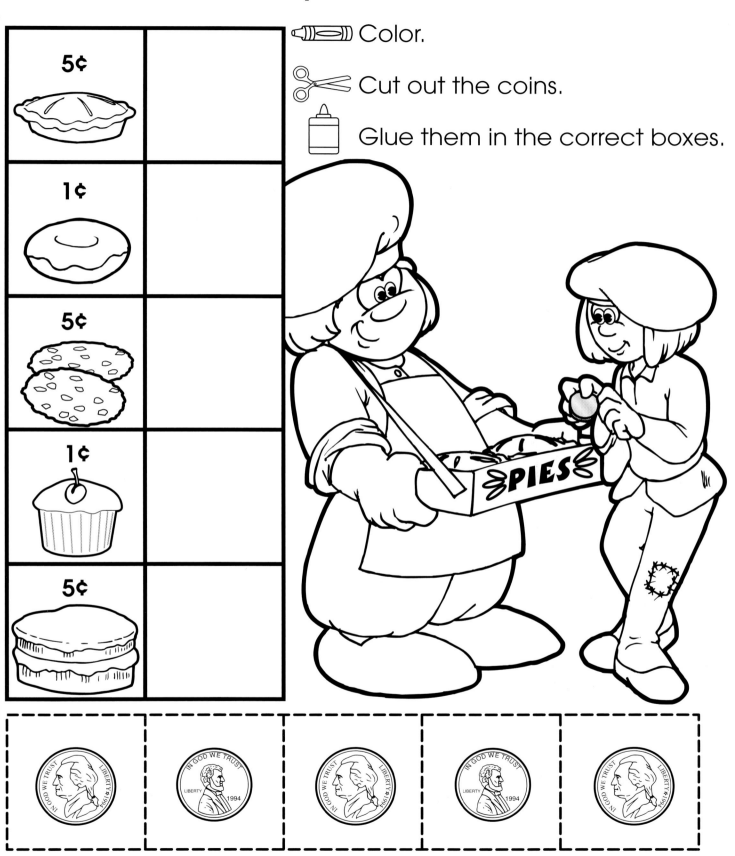

Color.

Cut out the coins.

Glue them in the correct boxes.

5¢

1¢

5¢

1¢

5¢

PIES

43

How To Use Page 45

1. Duplicate the page for each child.
2. Using the directions below (or create your own), have your students listen to and follow the directions as you read them aloud.

- *These children are looking at stars that show <u>opposites</u>. Here is an example of opposites—hot and cold.*
- *Put your finger on the first star. Do you see a sky at <u>night</u>?*
- *Now look at the stars at the bottom of the page. Find one that shows the sun. When would you see the sun? (Pause.) A day sky is the opposite of a <u>night</u> sky.*
- *Cut out that star and paste it next to the first star.*
- *Continue to find opposites for the other three stars.*

Finished Sample

Name _____

Twinkle, Twinkle, Little Stars

✂ Cut.

Glue to match the opposites.

How To Use Page 47

1. Duplicate the page for each child.
2. Have students read each color word; then color.

Finished Sample

Spider Shapes

Read.

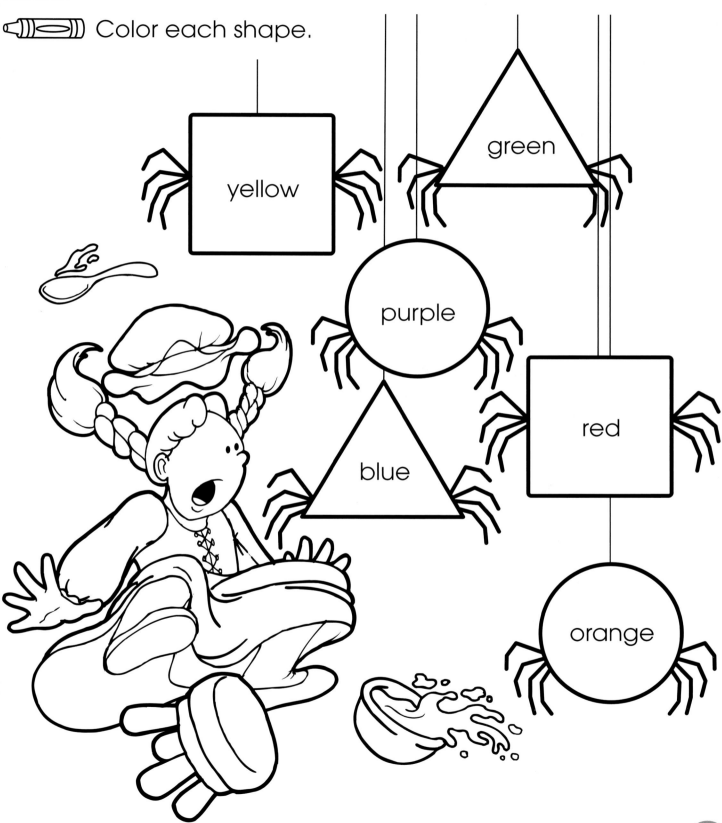 Color each shape.

Name _____

Rain, Rain, Go Away Rhymes

 Cut out the rhyming pictures.

 Glue them by the correct raindrop.

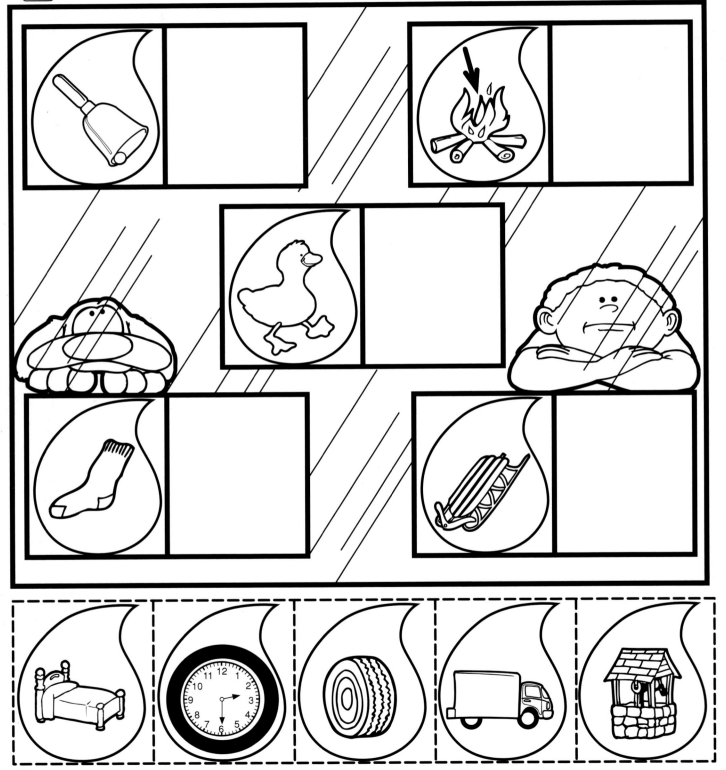